Secular Audacity

Secular Audacity

by Joy Gaines-Friedler

Copyright © 2025 by Joy Gaines Friedler

Published by   Mayapple Press
              362 Chestnut Hill Road
              Woodstock, NY 12498
              mayapplepress.com

ISBN 978-1-952781-26-1
Library of Congress Control Number 2025930402

Acknowledgements:
To the hard working editors of the following journals which originally found purpose & pleasure in this work: *Poetry East, Peninsula Poets, San Pedro River Review, Big Scream, 3rd Wednesday, Poetica Magazine, Panoply, Black Fork Review, Pink Panther, Poetry Super Highway, Jewish Literary Journal, Writer's Digest Magazine, Poets For Paris, Driftwood Review, Call & Response, Pulse, Lothorian, 101 Jewish Poems for the Third Millenium, A&U Magazine. Broadkill River Review, Vox Populi.*

Quotations from the work of Abraham Joshua Heschel are used with permission from Professor Susannah Heschel.

Cover design by Judith Kerman; cover art, detail of "Tänzerin mit blauem Rock (Dancer in Blue Skirt)," 1918, by Egon Schiele. Book designed and typeset by Judith Kerman with titles in Book Antiqua and text in Bell MT.

Contents

Introduction	9

I

Skin & Stone	13
Upon Answering the Question: Do You Believe in God?	14
Assisted Living / Caring for the Irreducible	15
Refusing to Ride *The Creator*	19
Children of Survivors	20
Days of Awe	22
My Mother Phones from Florida	23
The Polish Café	24
A Mother Story	26
Last Trip to the Barber	28
Counting Change	29
Confession of a Tree That Survived Bergen-Belsen	30
The Hebrew Word for *Mysticism* Is the Same as *To Receive*	31
Please Provide the Routing Number	32
The Construct of Order	33
Vigilance Notes: Sunday	34
Chevra Kadisha	35

II

At the Market in Akko—A Wedding	39
Jerusalem : At the Market in The Old City	41
The Gate of the Philosopher	42
A Bedouin Girl on a Cliff in Israel	43
New Year's Day	44
Let Me Be G-Flat Minor 7th	46
Recalling a Conversation with My Father...	48
Communion	49
Grief Again	51
Lake Michigan Sunset	52
Shabbat—New York City	53
Monarch Metamorphosis	54
Dictionary.com Says, *Things Are Buzzing*	55
Recycling Bibles	56

Philadelphia, 2017	58
Taking a Leap	59
May You Be Inscribed	60
It Seems	61
Guest Appearance	62
Disbelief in Numbers	64
About the Author	66
Acknowledgements & Thank You's	67

For Elissa

*Life-long friend &
most spiritually audacious person I know.*

Introduction

Deeply moved by the philosophy, theology and scholarship of Rabbi Abraham Joshua Heschel, I contacted his daughter, Professor Susannah Heschel, Distinguished Professor of Jewish Studies at Dartmouth College to ask permission to include her father as epigraphs on a number of poems in this collection. It is Rabbi Heschel's social consciousness that draws me to him, and to what he called, the Jewish prophecy of civil justice.

That social consciousness infused with an ecumenical approach brought Heschel and Dr. Martin Luther King together. In March 1965, Heschel responded to King's call for religious leaders to join the Selma to Montgomery March for Voting Rights.

Born in 1907 in Warsaw, Poland, Heschel received his PhD from the University of Berlin in 1933. Ordained there, he taught Adult Jewish Studies in Germany until 1938, when all Jews of Germany holding Polish passports were suddenly arrested, held, then deported. Packed into a train, Heschel was forced to stand for three days. Once in Poland, Jews were denied entry. They remained at the border in miserable conditions. Locals refused to provide food for them. Heschel was rescued by family.

Later, from London, in 1940 Heschel emigrated to the United States where he desperately tried (unsuccessfully) to get his mother and sister out of Nazi occupied Poland, and where, by then, my mother-in-law, a teenager in Poland, had received notice to pack one suitcase and "report" to a detention center: her school. Jews were no longer allowed to study. Their schools became their first prisons. Separated from her parents, ten brothers and sisters, her entire community, she begged her captors to let her go home. She and one brother were the only two who survived the Nazi holocaust.

How does one live in a world that's turned against you?

Like Heschel, my mother-in-law defiantly maintained a high estimation of the nature of humankind. Heschel became professor of Jewish Ethics and Mysticism at New York's Jewish Theological Seminary of

America, a post he held for the rest of his life. My mother-in-law sang in the kitchen so as not to bring sorrow or fear to her children.

Heschel acknowledged what he called the spark of the divine within each person. I feel this way about poetry too. Poems move us because they contain something marvelous; something that language itself cannot reach; something that cannot otherwise be expressed.

Like, Heschel, MLK, and my mother-in-law (who lived to 101), I too am driven by the notion of a collective responsibility. These poems are personal and universal. They speak from a secular mysticism in conversation with Heschel's pious views, but I believe, much to the same end.

I

The tree of knowledge grows upon the soil of mystery

— Rabbi Abraham Joshua Heschel

Skin & Stone

I've always believed in skin,
the way it bleeds when pricked

then repairs itself like a battlefield
gone to meadow. Chasing up and down

rudderless knuckles, your hands, mine—
this is how I learn Faith. Agonies

repaired by touch, by a word, and song.
Is there a difference between Belief

and the act of believing?
Just as he took his last breath my friend lay

upon her husband's body, not in fear
or distress, but the way I remember holding

a sun-warmed stone to my cheek
to feel its remaining heat.

And just as I couldn't forget Roger
who in fifth grade wouldn't stop loving me

because I was kind to him
when others couldn't be,

I remember a letter that came with an
unexpected thank you

and how I wished I could let that penetrate
my skin—but I knew it wouldn't

because so much of me is stone
trying hard not to be.

Upon Answering the Question: Do You Believe in God?

I can't answer that because
it doesn't matter to me.

But how do you explain all this?

An explanation is not important to me.

How do you explain Space?

As that thing that has no beginning
and no end.

But it had to start somewhere.

Why? Why is a beginning necessary?

How do you explain Beauty?

The same way you explain Suffering.

Don't you feel alone?

Yes. I do.

God's son died so that we may live!

Maybe Abraham was testing God, not
the other way around.

Assisted Living
Caring for the Irreducible

Our task is to let the divine emerge from our deeds.
—A. J. Heschel

I
Maybe we have practiced caring for them
the way we handle the heavy scrolls of Torah,
kiss them with our frail lips,
with our weighty book of prayers.

We discover our names in them, drape them
with breastplate, plait them in velvet.
They are scrolls scribed by their lives.
They hold all the shalts and shalt-nots inside them.
They are lifted heavily from their wheelchairs
then set down in their beds like something holy.

We memorize the Kaddish
then close the heavy curtains.

II
Two women in wheelchairs argue:

Don't touch me
What? Why?
Get away from me you idiot. I could kill you.

A timeless battle: One who wants only love.
One whose hard grief is a multitude of grief,
a stone box of grief.

III
I love thoughts and ideas, love music, love
these women silent or silenced by age
who sit in wheelchairs against the walls
like soldiers with no enemies, as though
past worries were vain indulgences. They sit
without husbands, those who held them at night,
their lives in frames along their dressers.
Dear God, a son, a daughter, a trip to Italy.

IV
The lady at the front desk wears Florida all over her.
She is hot pink and yellow and whispers to me,
Your mother is so happy to see you,
as though this secret is a key to unlock the past,
as though unlocking it would rewrite it.

Florida reminds me that I have curly hair,
that the ocean is its own planet,
that humans can recreate what should belong
only to cockroaches and very large spiders,
that I am often right and frequently wrong;
I love as simply as I despair
and feel too easily the suffering of others.
I know the secret to life is to make it through—
joy is one way. Velvet whispers of Torah another.

V
If one of the irreducible asks you
what floor she lives on
remember the way she once knew consolation
and to console, or drank rum and laughed heavily.
Tears are wreathed in dense beautiful layers. May we all
find acceptance in change. Amen.

VI
They are rows of trees lining the boulevard.
They are frail crystal cups.
They are collectors of small treasures.
They are the flat surface of blue water.
They are the western sky.

VII
Sunlight breaks through the heart here.
It can barely raise its head.

The small nurse with hands of a prophet claims,
*If I can make one of them happy
just for a moment—it's enough. Your mom…
smiles every morning. See? See it? That's what I get.*

VIII
There are two sides to this life:
The side you nurture, and the side you fail.
The child you inspire, and the one you reduce.
Sacrifice. And the women you turn hard against.

IX
Sometimes they get violent. Your mom though,
she always smiles.

X
Mom has a missing tooth. Her smile both warms
and concerns me. It was an implant, a single denture—
a thing she could never keep track of. Like her wedding band,
it's gone missing. Life is like this—grief for
the small lost things—joy in the not caring. The past
just wants to be the future.
The future cares little of the past.

XI
I am a seer and I walk into walls.
I put my right foot in front of my left,
push the button for the third floor,
push aside the smell of urine.
I hate my mother's missing buttons,
the stains on her pants. I'm sorry
I showed her a recent photo of herself—
her long, unreadable gaze—
What do you think? I asked her.
I should see a dentist, she said.

Does the Torah suggest the proper way
to respect someone else's prayer?

XII
These discoveries are not new to me.
In the small sheets of hospital beds I discovered
love is the devotee of suffering.
And when the doctor with eyebrows of palm trees,
and his disciples in white coats, entered the children's ward

like Moses—prayers rose up all over the place.
I became the mother child of all the children.
I became the mother child of my mother.
I have always been my mother's next day.

Refusing to Ride *The Creator*

My cousin wears a red bandanna, green tank top,
can't wait for the line to wing its way
to the metal pew she'll climb into
                          with faith. I refuse

to trust a track tended by a tattered man
who may be drunk.

I watch her ride her little kayak into the sky—
imagine the view from up there & fear
the fall.

I'm not brave. Not about this.

I've hitch-hiked through canyons,
gone off in cars rippling with danger
— been thrown around

by love & its escape. The view
from the river is just fine.

There is rocking, there is screaming, metal,
wheels, track, wind. Bruises.

Look how convinced she is
          that no matter how jostled,

there is cotton candy in the end.

Children of Survivors

> *It all happened so fast. The Ghetto. The Deportation. The sealed cattle car.*
> — *Elie Wiesel*

Everywhere we go
the trains
come with us.

The suitcases
they were ordered to pack
(a deception to keep their mothers calm)

they come with us...
those extra sweaters
they would never use.

We hide
among the ghosts
in small picture frames that survived.

Silent as tubers,

we asked for no more
than could be found
inside a box of Cracker Jacks,

said nothing
when on Halloween
our friends

dressed
as Hitler.

Whistles shook us awake too.
From dreams where we
were pregnant.

Everywhere we went
the dogs came
and herded us backward.

We clutched the locks of chains
even as the whistles faded.

Days of Awe

Days of reflection from Rosh Hashanah to Yom Kippur—the day in which we "afflict" our souls so that we may feel closest to our own sense of being.

September. The pool equipment stowed,
the mower returned to the shed. Tonight
quiet ascends like the silence after sirens.

Soon the moon will go missing. Soon the night birds
will call other night birds. Each call a small pledge.

Tonight I will ask my mother, who can
no longer remember if she's eaten or
who her friends are, if she remembers my father,

or recalls the way the earth evolves
beneath the unending cycles of the moon—
        the way what disappears is still there.

It is difficult to ask forgiveness.
Prayer, I think, is as much defiance as it is agreement.

Yes, she'll answer, *Oh sure.* Then,
I'm fine. I won't believe any of it. It's September.
We've started our migration inward
to bear the voice of repentance.

Like those night birds I will listen hard.

My Mother Phones from Florida

Your father is really something.
The police say he broke the guy's
expensive dental work. Your father
says the guy came at him
with a golf club in his hand...
that the guy was swearing.
Your father doesn't like to be cursed at,
you know, he has a thing about respect.
Anyway...Apparently...
your father hit the ball further
than anyone expected. Maybe
your father's impatience got the best of him,
maybe he didn't like the way the guy was...
dilly-dallying. Anyway...
your father claims that he went over there
to apologize but the guy came at him
with his curse words and his golf club,
so your father socked him in the mouth.
It was a WWII moment. War
on the golf course. All the guys his age
learned how to box, you know.
Anyway...the next thing you know
the police are at the door.
This was the excitement for today.
This is your father.
This is retirement in Florida.

The Polish Café

for Jack Myers

Reading the menu, I am dipping in and out
of an unforgiving feeling. I am smoke
disappearing then reappearing between
light and shadow. Self-conscious, dark haired,
I feel I'll be discovered, handed a yellow star, tattooed.

Maybe I'll order pierogi,
so much like my mother's kreplach,
dumplings stuffed with meat, and I think
of how the selling of kosher food became a crime;
how the butchers went missing,
how the locals spit in the ghetto wells.

And right here in this family restaurant
filled with smokers and drinkers I want to stand up
and yell. I want to tell the couple at the table next to me
that my mother was only thirteen for God's sake —
snatched away, thrown into a cattle car,
war put inside her,

that still, night whistles wake her
weeping for her mother transferred
like those dirty dishes to an extermination camp.

I can get crazy like this, let my imagination fill,
think I owe the dead something. Come on,
these hungry drinkers and smokers have nothing
to do with history except to live in the safety beyond it.

They're here to eat kielbasa.

The waitress holds a pen to pad, a menu under her arm.
Was it her mother who turned in my starving uncle—
watched him shot for trying to steal a potato
from her compost pile? And just when I'm thinking,
Christ,

the day's become a ripped shirt, a terrible hunger,
forgive, forgive, orders are orders, just order,
I notice above the bar a portrait of John Paul II,
his cotton face, his hand raised in a gesture of what?
Humility? Finite Distance? He blesses this place
as one who sees life in terms of them and us,
as one who comes out on top in the knowledge of that.

I consult my menu, smell nutmeg infused onion
and the repulsive stench of burning flesh.
I order potato pierogi without gravy, tell myself,
just finish your dinner and get out.

A Mother Story

1.
Begins with hands—long,
nails polished smooth.
Woman sequined, all curve and body.
Woman as Redbud, wide, full of flower.
You run your fingers over their firm surety.

2.
She is a tree beside a grove of trees.
When the sky closes around her
she becomes solemn, blameful—as if a deer
has snapped a branch from her.

3.
A birthday party. The knotty pine basement.
A blue circus cake. Pin-The-Tail-On-The-Donkey.
Disoriented by the spin, no one finds the proper spot.
No one can. She doesn't notice the donkey taped too high.

4.
You try but you can't escape her. Nor can you make her
crave what the sea infuses into the air, the bell whistle
of waves, the communal sound of muted birds.
She has no need for the sweetness of a child's mouth,
no craving for their voices. Hers is the night trains, cars
stuffed with human cargo. You point her to the clouds.
You ask her to find an image in them she can name.
She claims, *It's all so terrible*, leaving you dispersed
and shapeless.

5.
Your father moves her to Florida
where the sun acts on behalf of warmth.
You move to California, find you miss
the wail and siren of storms.

6.
You watch the long hands of the clock
confuse her days. You pay her bills, talk to doctors,
find her a companion. You find ways to make your mother safe.
She wants *her* mother now. They have taken away her phone.
She asks you, *How will I get home?*

Last Trip to the Barber

The road to the sacred leads through the secular.
—*A. J. Heschel*

As I drove my father, heron-frail, he
craned his neck into the wrinkled sky, said,

Sometimes I see the face of my father in the clouds.

This must be a trick—
the way what once stung me,
up close is actually
something delicate, with wings
and its own compound body.

I too looked up, seeking a sign—

— silence
fell between us.

Where did this untried trust come from?

and that look from the guys in the barber shop
when I held open the door
and they first saw him—

their eyes like startled cats
turned swiftly to contentment.

Your dad is an amazing guy, one of them said.

What we don't know, can't know,
might fill the sky.

Counting Change

As the sun rose this morning, my father died.

Now, nine at night, every light in the bedroom
glows white as herons at dusk tip-toeing into

unfamiliar-water. My mother is sitting on the edge

of their bed. She has emptied the contents
of a blue jar, calculating what's there, what's left.

I know that whatever my father left won't be enough.

Mom, I ask, *Do you believe in heaven?*

Not really, she answers without a penny's
worth of hesitation, without ever looking up.

Confession of a Tree That Survived Bergen-Belsen

The heart is often a lonely voice in the marketplace of living.
— *A. J. Heschel.*

I am made of silence.
It's been a kind of refuge.

The world, cruel as a borer,
I pretend to be brave which

helps me believe that I am.
I was not merely witness.

I too breathed in the smoke and ash,
while I held what souls I could,

until, I too was removed.

After the gathering of the few
who survived, I joined them

as we were smuggled through briar,
given false papers, unrooted, unwelcomed.

To live is to speak, to sing, to restore
what time teaches:

There is no such thing as secure.
Still, here I am. Replanted. Fully present.

Here I am, offering
some small flowers, fruit,

offering the wind a song
sung through my audacious leaves.

The Hebrew Word for *Mysticism* Is the Same as *To Receive*

In the parking lot between
brick buildings on campus

a girl dropped to the pavement
like a bird   shot.

Her body shimmied—a rain stick. Blood
from her lip.

The Hmong say simply of Epilepsy
   The spirit leaves you & you fall down.

I knelt beside her. Took her hand.

I considered the soul—
how it is *attached* to us,
how, even after death it remains

present, hangs around
not yet ready to leave the body behind—

         what grief it must be to lose such a bond.

I don't know how I knew
to sit on the pavement and wait,
stroke her hand. *It's okay. It's okay. You're okay.*

Thinking she must hate this fate, while
we waited for her spirit to return.

Her body calmed. Her eyes opened.
I sat with her. She stared up at me.

Please Provide the Routing Number

The lady says—*hospital in Florida.*
Says, *You pay your mother's bills. Correct?*

Your mother has agreed to pay all expenses
for your brother—who is here without insurance.

Your mother has given us her credit card.
She has maxed the limit.

We need her checking account number please.

Ask the fishermen how quickly to construct a net.
Ask the zookeeper about a wall. Put a tiger behind it.

No—I won't. No. She won't. I repeat.

But, there was an admittance window,
two chairs, your brother, your mother.
She signed an agreement.

Ask the daughter how to protect her mother. Repeat.

She will not. She will not pay his bills.

Dementia—I say, with the slow stride of
the tiger. Then, *I have a lawyer.*

The Construct of Order

> *God manifests himself in events rather than in things.*
> —A. J. Heschel

I pull off the road at the sound of the cell phone.

Through the windshield, clothes dry on a line.
I close one eye then switch to the other,
play with perspective, watch an entire house

disappear. The tiger carries with it
all the fights of its father, all the brutal,
necessary killings. Old love wicks through

the cleaned, then cleaned again carpets. And now,
as spring struts around half naked, I'm fatigued
by leaves that grow like speed freaks and

memory loss. As soon as I hang up I'll phone Hospice,
use frequent flyer miles to get back to Florida.
For now, like the invisible hands of memory,

the pegged clothes flag in the wind.

Vigilance Notes: Sunday

The greatest insights happen to us in moments of awe.
—*A.J. Heschel*

That heron needn't notice
the star-shaped blooms it walks in,
flowers adored by butterflies who,
with their keratin wings,
risk everything
to be here.

It needn't notice that pair of mourning doves
weaving a nest beside that blue wall,
their shadows
so much larger than themselves.

Does it notice that in the distance
the intercoastal bridges
are timed to open
in perfect succession?

My mother never learned to drive
depended always on my father
who took her to the beauty shop;
the grocery store. He waited for her
in waiting rooms.

What primal desire
does it take to build a nest?

As my mother slips further,
blinds already closed on this world,
I whisper in her ear, *bravo, Ma—
for holding out one more day.* Tomorrow
the sun will rise on the anniversary
of my father's death. Again,
those drawbridges will open
to let another tall-masted boat pass through.

Chevra Kadisha
A Holy Society

As I enter the building for my mother's funeral
a woman in white head-wrap, long skirt,
is thanking me.

The first person I see, she is
a heron; her voice a psalm.
She is the opening liturgy of the day.

Thank you, she repeats, for allowing me
to care for your mother. *Tahara*,
the ritual of cleansing the body, of spiritual bathing

—it is her job, this privilege.

Mine is over.

If, as they say, we are descendants of a single life,
then caring for one is caring for all.

My mother can no longer
repay such a kindness as this—

You're welcome I say,

believing in none of it. And all of it.

II

The highest peak of spiritual living…lies wherever we are, and may be ascended in a common deed.

—Abraham Joshua Heschel

At the Market in Akko — A Wedding

I should have no arguments with the hijab;
still, it disturbs me.

Sometimes it's hard to be American,
full of independence,
        giddy with liberty.

You Americans have no idea
what it's like to constantly feel threatened.

I think: A Constitution requires protection.
The Melting Pot separates
as easily as water sifts through silt.

I want to go to the man selling mangos,
ask if he hurled rocks during the
last *uprising*, or worse,

planned the strapping of explosives
to the bodies of young men.

Then I think of the hard news from home:

Dr. Tiller, killed during a Sunday morning service
in his church in Kansas. From what
do we gain pride?

I turn to my nephews, young
Israeli soldiers, ask if the army
teaches them to hate. They both say no,

and I'm more confused than ever.

I hear the movement of wings. Doves.
I search for their perch when suddenly

…singing, rhythmic clapping rings
against these ancient passages, these stone walls.

Men dance around a groom dressed in red—
on a golden draped workhorse.

Women in head cover follow.
They too, dance. They too, sing.

As they pass me, me with my silly camera,
one gestures for me to join them. Join them.
She takes my hand.
She pulls me in.

Jerusalem : At the Market in The Old City

A small woman
In the clothes of Poland
Before the darkness
Before the heart tattooed
   with its grief
Schmatahs
My mother calls them.
Ragged, patched together,
Reclaimed.
She is wearing her exile,
Her lost mother's
Memory, her flag of
Small comfort.

Whatever happened—
Keeps happening.

Keeps her from escaping
The night howl of train whistles.

Her smile keeps clean
The golden stone of Jerusalem.

She is holding
A single bill in one hand,
Buying macaroons,
Something sweet for the table.

The Gate of the Philosopher

Inspired by The Artist Looks at Nature, *1943,
Surrealist painting by Charles Sheeler*

The gate opens to perennial fields.

Opens to a garden of theories
and water mining its own path.

Opens to a house made of windows.

A tree is never just a tree
but the language born of its roots.

The sky isn't merely sky
but the awesome limitlessness of it.

There are yews growing in cement.
There are shadows skewing logic
and perspective. The Philosopher knows

there is no such thing as green.

The gate is open to a plein air man
painting self-portraits on walls he invents.

As Rabbi Heschel says, *we are free
against our will. And have the audacity*

to choose. Rarely do we know how or why.

A Bedouin Girl on a Cliff in Israel

Wearing a blood red quabbeh around her chest
and hips. Red against the skeleton of a rusted

pickup truck. Red against tank beige sand
and Mediterranean blue. A Canaanite

Goddess she walks in sandals toward the edge
of the bluff overlooking the busy highway.

Her arm extended, she is holding something out
in front of her, holding it away from her

as though its stench will taint her.
She is holding a dead cat by its hind legs.

She has done this before. From the highway,
I watch her walk to the edge. In Israel

there are worlds that never meet. As the car reaches
the bluff—I crane my neck to look up. She

is beautiful. She is holding a dead cat.
I watch her let it let go.

New Year's Day

Last night's candles are cold & misshapen.
The little lights around the bar burn still.

I gave in to celebration long before midnight,
then woke at dawn to the sound of an owl.

I hope the owl's call is answered by another—
that her answer fills the cavity he lives in.

Snow falls a capella, Gregorian,
while my head throbs like the pulse & pound

of pots & pans, the metal spoon taken outside
at midnight when I was ten, a strange kid

who believed no one notices the trees
but me, who dreamed of a house with no dark

hallways. No booby-traps. Where I imagined a man
—yes, a kind of savior

whose touch could create an Eden in the new air.
But mine is a theology of the common deed.

Beyond the stag-head trees, a house, its roof
covered in fresh snow, patches of heat

escape & the word *Go*, or *God*, or
it could be *Dog* melts into it.

Mine is a theology of radical amazement,
where nature & order are not an end-stop,

but a *Why?* The way *go*, or *god* or *dog* on a rooftop
is both eloquent and funny. I have faith

the old trees will survive another year
so that I might receive their endless missives.

I'm hopeful & frightened at the same time.
There is a clutch of secrets held silent

in the overnight snow. Birds are busy at the feeders.
Trees are my prophets—I am a disciple of their shadows.

Let Me Be G-Flat Minor 7th

> *A Mitzvah is like a musical score.... It is not enough to play the notes; one must be what he plays. One must live what he does.*
> —A. J. Heschel

Blue throw folded over the piano bench,
fat-belly ceramic cat holds open the pages.
The brass lamp moons hinged light

over steadfast notes, language
one reads
but cannot speak.

I know this song by heart,

know it in my body so fully it surges,
like the heave of wild flowers before the trees
leaf out, or the way the clock gives away

its next second, harmony
expelled—fully chorded
the way we hum our knowings,
                      our *uh-huh's*
to one another, deep-throated
and from the diaphragm—
the body, the body involved.

Oh! Let that one flat note
be the one that warms the world.
Let it make a temple of me.

Let it make a hallelujah a hallelujah.
Let it be the friend I always imagine,
that brings tea to the table
        with her *remember when's;*

that minor chord
heard in the wind along the river
and in the play area at the mall

where the children know nothing
of sorrow, but watch one another
like clues to a scavenger hunt.

We all start small—three fingered,
add a fourth, & no matter
the snow plow didn't show up,

no matter the doorbell lost its ring—
this chord resonates everything
we hold from the past,
a message from the future: *Listen. Listen.*

Be the giver of song.

Recalling a Conversation with My Father About Judaism and Its Unestablished *Heaven & Hell* — While He Helped Me with My Math

The dining room table
newspaper strewn—

Do we believe in heaven?

The concept, my father tells me
is not developed.

For us—the model is life:
The burden of the ant.

The way dust settles
but the memory of it lingers.

Our model is the hoisting of the flag
by those soot covered firemen.

For us, afterlife is unexplained;

better you should worry
about getting your homework done.

I remember those story problems—
how embarrassed I was

by my inability to form a reckoning
while others had no problem

establishing the equation.
I needed to know more.

The train going x?
          With whom? —Where?

Communion

> *I'm injecting Interferon in my stomach—taking the pills*
> *and DDI—Jesus, what an array.*
> —James Kerr

Our last conversation, you said,
that all your life   you'd been *a shadow.*

Then you said,
it is time for this to end

and shocked me
with   *pray for me.*

I thought of our ritual of passing around the bong
on Sunday mornings, how you called it
Morning Mass,

and the Communion I took
while attending church with you one day
    surprised by the way the wafer melted in my mouth

before I returned to kneel next to your laughing shoulders,
    your eyes a bit scared for my brazen Jewish soul.

Before you slipped away from me
      I wanted to remind you

how fun it was to slide Kahlua into our coffee,
dance to Stairway to Heaven, stay up all night

talking about God and fathers   —how, despite the lesions
and new words like, *lesions,*
      and *pneumatoid,*

I will always feel the stone warmth of you.

I am glad that your death eyes were 3000 miles away,
that it was your mother who was there to look into them,
telling you to let go,
and I am sorry that it was not me.

I'm thinking,
maybe I will lie and say that
I held the hand of my best friend as he died from AIDS,

which I do—only it isn't a lie.

Grief Again
for Mike

Every turn that summer
pressed me deeper into the singularity of it.
Morning coffee in hand—

a long slatted boardwalk, my feet repeating
its coda: *solid, denuded, solid, denuded.*

Cherries ripened on the tree.
Birds brought their broods to the feeders.
The beach grasses grew tall.

By Fall their sway, like cello song, sorrowful,
yet fully alive.

That is the irony of Grief.

Ghostly houses of memory
light along the shore.

I think of him now
in the memory of dark beer & carryout boxes;
the way the tide gives itself over—absorbs,
then reflects the changing light.

All summer I found myself, not at the water's edge
looking out, but on the water itself,
facing those houses.

Lake Michigan Sunset

Everything's gone silent
as though a group of doctors has entered
                               the children's ward.

Drone of water vehicles stowed,
a couple strolls the long edge of conversation.

Waves, like fear, have subsided—
only their small breaths remain.

A congregation of gulls passes overhead.
I stop counting at ten groups of ten.
I stopped counting long ago,

days absent from school, then returning
soundless as a sunset. There were sicker kids—
a boy from fire, patched with skin grafts;

a girl who walked metal, in metal braces. I wonder
where that seagull is, the one with only one leg.
Amazing how it keeps up. Does it teach me
something I already know?

Everything has gone quiet. Hushed.
As though the Chaplain has arrived.

Lost shovels and forgotten tee-shirts
lie unsaved. In another place
an orchestra has begun its evening tuning.

The sun is sinking. It touches the edge of a wound.

Shabbat — New York City

> *The meaning of the Sabbath is to turn from the results of creation to the mystery of creation; from the world of creation to the creation of the world.*
> —*A. J. Heschel*

There are people who live
entirely without community
a friend told me as I walked with him
down 5th Ave. to Shul.
He didn't notice

my lack of uniform, unpaid dues,
didn't notice my non-conformity,
my well-groomed flight feathers,
my refugee status, my preference
for quiet places. He didn't notice
my rent checks.

Maybe I never let myself
be a part of anything
that would remind me that
I've never been a part of anything.

His community forms around ritual
that depends on a certain hour
of the day and the New Moon.

Mine is the observance
of the day itself.

Sometimes we seek blindly
what we need, without
knowledge or intent. I told him.

I didn't walk through the door he held open for me.
Instead, I got on a bus with strangers—
sought familiarity in their congregation.

Monarch Metamorphosis
for Linda

We watch them grow gorgeous
in their striped summer shirts
their blind-eye canes of antennae.

Mornings I take my coffee outside,
examine each leaf. Search for them.
Seek their preservation.

My beautiful friend was killed—
there is no other way to say it—
by the man who once sat with her

in the shade of their chalk maple. Gone
too. Drought sensitive. Anxious
about the caterpillars' survival, my search
is the single inseparable constant of my life.

I keep hoping for a chrysalis,
push myself toward the next stage.

At ten, I'd never seen milkweed.
Never seen a gun.

How do any of us survive?

Dictionary.com Says, *Things Are Buzzing*

says the word of the day is
Paparazzo, which made it

into the dictionary after Fellini's
La Dolce Vita included a character
by that name, Paparazzo, who took snapshots
of beautiful women.

Maybe I wanted to be one of those women,
bikini-clad and waving from the rooftop—

waving at a helicopter floating a statue of Jesus
all over the city.

Maybe Fellini's Paparazzo is another poet
looking to capture what words cannot.

Or a cynic looking to sell to the lowest
bidder, another bit of low-brow culture
my lit teacher calls *postmodern*.

(I wonder how we can be living
in the modern "now" and be beyond it
at the same time.)

A friend says
"We are *reborn* each day."
Seems painful— all that resurrection.

Yet, each morning my skin feels firm,
smooth, something that persists, pursues even—
something buzzing.

Recycling Bibles

The Hebrew word for "Prayer" (Tefillah) connotes "thinking truth" & requires "judgement of oneself"—making prayer personal.

Two men in white shirts, black trousers

stand
      the proper footage away

handing out pocket bibles
on campus.

Some things need no reminding—

the way I'm grateful for my curly hair,
or for my cat who never resents my accidental steps

(all he craves is connection).

It's been too long since I let
Leonard Cohen's hallelujahs
wash over me,   let the moon be a reminder

of something I've always loved—the moon,
the color blue for example,
         or the way
hitting a tennis ball cleanly   feels good,

better, even, than winning.

A guy I know wears a button that reads
Shun the Non-Believers.   Really? I asked—

You would really do that?

A crime is a crime, he answered.

There are pocket bibles abandoned
all over the Student Center
on tables & couches—the fireplace.

I pick them up—find the recycling, rather than the trash.

It's personal.

Philadelphia, 2017

> *Two days in February: 100 tombstones toppled in Philadelphia, 170 in St. Louis, 11 bomb threats against Jewish community centers around the nation. In August, Unite The Right Rally, Charlottesville, Virginia. Then… Pittsburgh, 2018, Tree of Life Synagogue, 11 dead, 6 wounded.*

Volunteers helped lift
the fallen tombstones
at the Jewish cemeteries

while we were seated
at the table feeling recovered
from the history of shattered glass.

That night jittery,
a dream reoccurred:

We were outside in the dark,
calling home on our cell phones
when 100 leafless trees fell around us.

The soil turned hard as granite, unplantable,
still we walked. We walked through
what we thought was old debris.

But look, you said, *the trees are stricken
with borers, infested, it's not safe out here.*

Let's go in, you said.
And we did.

Yet, we were still outside.

Taking a Leap

To the Biblical mind in its radical amazement, nature, order, is not an answer but a problem: Why is there order, why being at all?
—*A. J. Heschel*

I'm making my world smaller—

finding Beauty in the faceless
butterfly—all wings & feelers,
conspicuous flight;

a little laugh at the wild turkey antics
around the neighbor's deck;

a note on the sidewalk
that reads simply,
    Yes.

I'm taking a leap around the devastated
islands—trying not to breathe in fumes & ash,
the acres of fire—I refuse to be consumed
by the wild things seeking escape.

The sonnet they say is the music of love.
I'm listening. I'm listening. *Yes.*

I'm making my world smaller—

eggplant & rosemary, red grapes,
or maybe just peanut butter & jelly for dinner.

May You Be Inscribed

*The Book of Life records all people considered Righteous.
At Rosh Hashanah one prays not to be removed from its pages.*

The year starts in metaphor—
God crossing out names. Still,
like the new moon, what seems lost
is still there.

The way a scar is a reminder of what was.

My hands are labeled:

> knuckle burns
> (the searing elements)
> finger numb from the too sharp knife.

Really, they are wrinkles of wisdom.

This morning I made a list
of all my lost ones.

Even those never born.

This morning, a magazine, a photo
of The Bridge Keepers
        who risk their lives to repair bonds
made of grass, woven by hand.

It must be terrifying
to stand on a threadbare bridge—

water rushing beneath. Yet they do it.

They grow up believing in what will hold.

It Seems

for Jim

only three years ago
we began our goodbyes.

Pray for me you asked, and I

had no idea how, or if I did,
what it might accomplish.

Instead I heard myself wish a good journey
as together we listened to the call
of a cactus wren.

But it wasn't three years ago—
today marks thirty years since

I walked that trail in Sabino Canyon,
insects buzzing their work ethic,

hawks bunting high against heaven,
and placed a granite nugget in my pocket

to lay beside the other miracles I collect;
nests, feathers, driftwood.

I will lay a stone on your stone,
I had promised. Although I never said it.

I waited for you, while you slept virused,
fevered, as the hills went deep water blue,

the sky blood red, then turquoise.
You woke as the desert gave up its heat.

In all these years, it's that blue halo of Tucson sky
I remember most, as though that light we sat in,

and the memory of it, is the prayer
you asked for. The thing you sought.

Guest Appearance
    Oct. 7, 2023

I had a small, non-speaking part,
a morning call in the massacre scene.
Five hours—I was made to walk in circles,
pace the floor, check the clock.

The scene was full color, sound, and soundless.
Fields of guava, the houses burned. Children fled; a festival
of music played in the background then went blade silent.
Their blood disappeared into the sand.

They hired extras to do the slaughtering & later
to pour in through the breached borders to steal
laptops & the kids' bikes.

In the end, grenade pins sparkled in the desert sun
outside the packed-then-blown-to-pieces shelters,
        miles of machine-gunned cars,
           (drivers plastered against glass & rubber),
        babies killed in their cribs & bunk beds,
        parents forced to watch, then slaughtered
        in their pajamas.

In the burnt acreage, the exhaust stench of motorcycles
carrying hostages west hummed with the distant sound
of approaching tanks & drones.

Critics immediately weighed in; it was too bloody;
it wasn't bloody enough. They couldn't tell

who were the enemy, who, the innocent.

Audiences were told *none of what you saw is real.*
They were slaughtering lambs for the festival
of harvest. It was all made up
in order that war crime could meet war crime.

My part was played from home—standing in my kitchen
standing, sitting, standing, checking my husband's face,
he checking mine.

Disbelief in Numbers

The glory of man is not in his will to power but in his power of compassion.
—*A. J. Heschel*

A storm of fallen apples—
bruised beneath the trees.

And another phone call from another friend
who says—it's bad
                    I'm losing hope.

I am unlike the pious
whose precepts prevent disbelief.

I arrive home to orange caution tape
around fallen limbs and wires.

There are apples
bruised beneath the trees.

I will take them in.
I will cut away their damage.

About the Author

After twenty years as a professional photographer, Joy Gaines-Friedler turned her lens to the written page. *Secular Audacity* is her sixth book of poetry. Her previous book, *Capture Theory*, was a Finalist for the Forward Indies Best Book of the Year Award. Among other recognitions and awards, Ms. Gaines-Friedler's manuscript *Stone on Your Stone* was co-winner of the 2021 Friends of Poetry/Celery City Chapbook Poetry Prize. Her work is also included in the anthology *101 Jewish Poems for the Third Millennium* and has received multiple nominations for both the Pushcart Prize and Best of The Net.

A graduate of Ashland University Ms. Gaines-Friedler holds an MFA in Creative Writing. She has taught for community colleges and universities, as well as many non-profit organizations that include literary arts programs and programs servicing at-risk communities in prisons, shelters, and asylum homes. She currently teaches workshops in memoir and poetry both online and in her home in Farmington Hills, Michigan.

Acknowledgements & Thank You's

Heschel quotes from: *The Wisdom of* Heschel, Third Printing, Farrar, Straus, and Giroux, NY, 1986. Thank you, Professor Susannah Heschel, Chair of the Judaic Studies Program at Dartmouth College.

Epigraph, *Children of Survivors*: Elie Wiesel. From his Acceptance Speech, on the occasion of the award of the Nobel Peace Prize in Oslo, December 10, 1986.

Thank you to Judith Kerman, publisher (Mayapple Press), poet, clown, musician, artist. Judith's multiple talents include spot-on design & editing. I cannot thank her enough.

Gratitude for your friendship, wisdom, & care with my work over the years: Susannah Sheffer & Elizabeth Solsnik. To Jack Ridl & all you good people in Jack's Landscapes group. To Barb Saunier & Chris Rhein.

Special shout-out to Stephen Mack Jones for believing in this book & waving from across the street to come talk to him about it. *Get it out*, he said. Also, to Gerry LaFemina for encouraging the same. Thank you.

Thank you to my memoir students past & present, most of whom love when I include poetry as a source of inspiration & craft. Such good souls they all are, writing brilliantly from their hearts. And to my private students, marvelous poets & friends, Alexander Morgan & Derek Daniels.

Special gratitude to Rabbi Abraham Joshua Heschel who helped me feel as though my fingers were praying.

Finally, to my husband, Moti Friedler. We suffered through the massacre that terrifying day, waiting to hear the fate of our family on Kibbutz Nir Oz. We never stop hoping for the return of our hostages, a full cease-fire, and an end to the horrific destruction & death of innocent Palestinians, Lebanese, Ukrainians & others. Heschel saw war as an act of violence against god. He claimed god was in search of man, not the other way around.

Recent Titles from Mayapple Press...

Ellen Stone, *Everyone Wants To Keep the Moon Inside Them*, 2025
    Paper, 90pp, $21.95
    ISBN: 978-1-952781-24-7

Lisken Van Pelt Dus, *How Many Hands to Home*, 2025
    Paper, 78pp, $20.95
    ISBN: 978-1-952781-23-0

David Michael Nixon, *A Wolf Comes to My Window*, 2024
    Paper, 40pp, $18.95
    ISBN: 978-1-952781-22-3

Zilka Joseph, *Sweet Melida*, 2024
    Paper, 60pp, $19.95
    ISBN: 978-1-952781-19-3

Eleanor Lerman, *Slim Blue Universe*, 2024
    Paper, 68pp, $20.95
    ISBN: 978-1-982781-17-9

Cati Porter, *Small Mammals*, 2023
    Paper, 78pp, $19.94 plus s&h
    ISBN 978-1-952781-15-5

Eleanor Lerman, *The Game Cafe*, 2022
    Paper, 160pp, $22.95 plus s&h
    ISBN 978-1-952781-13-1

Goria Nixon-John, *The Dark Safekeeping*, 2022
    Paper, 92pp, $19.85 plus s&h
    ISBN: 978-1-952781-11-7

Nancy Takacs, *Dearest Water*, 2022
    Paper, 84pp, $19.95 plus s&h
    ISBN: 978-1-952781-09-4

Zilka Joseph, *In Our Beautiful Bones*, 2021
    Paper, 108pp, $19.95 plus s&h
    ISBN: 9780-1-952781-07-0

Ricardo Jesús Mejías Hernández, tr. Don Cellini,
Libro de Percances/Book of Mishaps, 2021
    Paper, 56pp, $18.95 plus s&h
    ISBN: 978-952781-05-6

For a complete catalog of Mayapple Press publications, please visit our website at *mayapplepress.com*. Books can be ordered direct from our website with secure on-line payment using PayPal, or by mail (check or money order). Or order through your local bookseller.

www.ingramcontent.com/pod-product-compliance
Lightning Source LLC
Chambersburg PA
CBHW050044080526
44586CB00014B/1453